THE FIFTH DIMENSION

STUDY GUIDE

Copyright © 2024 by N. Charles Olmeda, PH.D.

Published by AVAIL

All rights reserved. No portion of this book may be reproduced, stored in a retrieval system, or transmitted in any form or by any means—electronic, mechanical, photocopy, recording, scanning, or other—except for brief quotations in critical reviews or articles, without prior written permission of the author.

Unless otherwise noted, all Scripture quotations are taken from the New King James Version®. Copyright © 1982 by Thomas Nelson. Used by permission. All rights reserved. | Scripture quotations marked ESV are from The ESV® Bible (The Holy Bible, English Standard Version®), copyright © 2001 by Crossway, a publishing ministry of Good News Publishers. Used by permission. All rights reserved. | Scripture quotations marked NASB are taken from the (NASB®) New American Standard Bible®, Copyright © 1960, 1971, 1977, 1995, 2020 by The Lockman Foundation. Used by permission. All rights reserved. www.lockman.org | Scripture quotations marked NIV are taken from the Holy Bible, New International Version®, NIV®. Copyright © 1973, 1978, 1984, 2011 by Biblica, Inc.™ Used by permission of Zondervan. All rights reserved worldwide. www.zondervan.com. The "NIV" and "New International Version" are trademarks registered in the United States Patent and Trademark Office by Biblica, Inc.™ | Scripture quotations marked NLT are taken from the Holy Bible, New Living Translation, copyright © 1996, 2004, 2015 by Tyndale House Foundation. Used by permission of Tyndale House Publishers, Inc., Carol Stream, Illinois 60188. All rights reserved.
For foreign and subsidiary rights, contact the author.

Cover design by: Sara Young
Cover photo by: Andrew van Tilborgh

ISBN: 978-1-962401-57-9   1 2 3 4 5 6 7 8 9 10

Printed in the United States of America

STUDY GUIDE

THE FIFTH DIMENSION

N. CHARLES OLMEDA, PH.D.

CONTENTS

Introduction 6

CHAPTER 1. Where It All Begins 14

CHAPTER 2. Come Out! Come Out Wherever You Are! 20

CHAPTER 3. Unexpected Dreams 26

CHAPTER 4. Misunderstood 32

CHAPTER 5. Time Is Your Best Friend 38

CHAPTER 6. When Failure Becomes Part of the Process 46

CHAPTER 7. When Betrayal Becomes Part of the Process 52

CHAPTER 8. Failure Is Not the End 58

CHAPTER 9. When Time Betrays 64

CHAPTER 10. Living With Failure and Success 70

CHAPTER 11. It's Only a Taste 78

CHAPTER 12. On a Dime 84

CHAPTER 13. Can You Be Trusted? 90

CHAPTER 14. Don't Settle 96

CHAPTER 15. Uncomfortable Places 102

CHAPTER 16. Finish What You've Started 110

CHAPTER 17. Number Two Person in a Number One World ... 116

CHAPTER 18. Sacrifice 122

CHAPTER 19. The Darkest Moment 128

CHAPTER 20. One More Act of Obedience 134

CHAPTER 21. It Was Worth the Process 142

CHAPTER 22. Greater Than *Your* Dream 148

CHAPTER 23. Whose Dream Is It Anyway? 154

CHAPTER 24. Forgetting the Pain 160

CHAPTER 25. Ready for Another Cycle? 166

Call to Salvation 172

THE FIFTH DIMENSION

UNVEILING THE PATH TO FULFILLMENT AND BEYOND

N. CHARLES OLMEDA, PHD

INTRODUCTION

Never live in such a rush that you can't take time to determine where you are.

READING TIME

As you read the Introduction of *The Fifth Dimension*, reflect on, and respond to the text by answering the following questions.

REFLECT AND TAKE ACTION:

What personal experience from the introduction resonates most with your own journey of feeling lost or unsure about your path?

_____
_____
_____
_____
_____
_____
_____

Have you ever experienced a moment where you thought you knew where you were headed, only to realize you were on the wrong path? What did you learn from that experience?

_____
_____
_____
_____
_____
_____
_____
_____

> *"For I know the plans I have for you," declares the Lord. "Plans to prosper you and not to harm you, plans to give you a hope and a future!"*
>
> —Jeremiah 29:11 (NIV)

Consider the scripture above and answer the following questions:

How have you experienced the truth of Jeremiah 29:11 in your own life? In what area are you still waiting to see this promise fulfilled?

_____
_____
_____
_____
_____
_____
_____

How can you cultivate trust in God's plan even when the path ahead is unclear?

_____
_____
_____
_____
_____
_____
_____

Meditate on Psalm 143:8 (NIV): *"Let the morning bring me word of your unfailing love, for I have put my trust in you. **Show me the way I should go, for to you I entrust my life.**"* How well do you trust God with your life? Explain.

In what ways does the metaphor of dimensions as the path toward the fulfillment of God-size dreams resonate with you?

_____
_____
_____
_____
_____
_____
_____
_____

How do you tend to handle the cycle of highs and lows in your pursuit of your dreams? Is it serving you or working against you? How so?

_____
_____
_____
_____
_____
_____
_____
_____

Why do you think it is so important to identify your current dimension in discerning God's purpose in your life?

___

In John 10:10 (BSB), Jesus says that *"the thief comes only to steal and kill and destroy. I have come that they may have life and have it in all its fullness."* What is the enemy stealing, killing, or destroying in your life today? What would it look like to have life to the full in those areas?

___

1ST DIMENSION

DREAMS & VISIONS

CHAPTER 1

WHERE IT ALL BEGINS

God-size visions and dreams have little to do with the end goal, although that matters, but everything to do with the transformative journey on your way to the goal.

READING TIME

As you read Chapter 1: "Where It All Begins" in *The Fifth Dimension*, reflect on, and respond to the text by answering the following questions.

REFLECT AND TAKE ACTION:

Are there dreams in your life that you have stopped pursuing? If so, why did you stop, and what would it take for you to revisit those dreams?

_____
_____
_____
_____
_____
_____
_____
_____
_____

Reflect on a dream you once had that didn't turn out as you expected. How did that outcome impact your belief in pursuing other dreams?

_____
_____
_____
_____
_____
_____
_____
_____
_____

> "Joseph had a dream, and when he told it to his brothers, they hated him all the more."
>
> —Genesis 37:5 (NIV)

Consider the scripture above and answer the following questions:

Is there a dream or goal you've shared with others that was met with resistance or criticism? How did that experience affect you?

_____
_____
_____
_____
_____
_____
_____
_____

When you encounter opposition to your dreams, do you find yourself withdrawing or trying harder? How does that reaction shape the outcome of your pursuits?

_____
_____
_____
_____
_____
_____
_____
_____

In what ways have you bound yourself to the pains and failures of your past? What would it look like to release them and move forward with the God-size dreams God has placed in your heart?

_____
_____
_____
_____
_____
_____
_____

Psalm 27:13 (NLT) says, *"Yet I am confident **I will see the LORD's goodness** while I am here in the land of the living."* In what area of your life are you struggling to believe that God's goodness will prevail?

_____
_____
_____
_____
_____
_____
_____

Consider how you define success. Do your personal definitions align with God's idea of success, as suggested in this chapter? If not, how could you recalibrate your expectations?

_____
_____
_____
_____
_____

_____

_____

_____

John 15:7-8 (NIV) tells us, *"If you remain in me and my words remain in you, ask whatever you wish, and it will be done for you. **This is to my Father's glory, that you bear much fruit,** showing yourselves to be my disciples."* What desires or requests have you been hesitant to bring before God? How might this be an obstacle to bearing good fruit?

_____

_____

_____

_____

_____

_____

_____

Think of a time when you felt ill-equipped to pursue a big dream or goal. How did you respond to those feelings of inadequacy, and what did you learn from the experience?

_____

_____

_____

_____

Consider Genesis 12:1-4 (NIV): *"The LORD had said to Abram, 'Go from your country, your people and your father's household **to the land I will show you. I will make you into a great nation**, and **I will bless you;** I will make your name great, and **you will be a blessing.** I will bless those who bless you, and whoever curses you I will curse; and all peoples on earth will be blessed through you.' So **Abram went, as the LORD had told him**; and Lot went with him. Abram was seventy-five years old when he set out from Harran."* What is God calling you to leave behind—whether a comfort zone, relationship, or personal identity—so that you can step into the promise He has prepared for you? What fears, excuses, or attachments are holding you back from taking that first step?

CHAPTER 2

COME OUT! COME OUT WHEREVER YOU ARE!

When your personal limitations end, God's unlimited possibilities begin.

READING TIME

As you read Chapter 2: "Come Out! Come Out Wherever You Are!" in *The Fifth Dimension*, reflect on, and respond to the text by answering the following questions.

REFLECT AND TAKE ACTION:

What comfort zones are currently holding you back from stepping into new opportunities or challenges? How have these familiar places limited your growth?

_____
_____
_____
_____
_____
_____
_____
_____
_____

What do you feel God urging you to release? What emotions surface when you consider letting go of those things?

_____
_____
_____
_____
_____
_____
_____
_____
_____

> "He took him outside and said, 'Look up at the sky and count the stars—if indeed you can count them.' Then he said to him, 'So shall your offspring be.' Abram believed the LORD, and he credited it to him as righteousness."
>
> **—Genesis 15:5-6 (NIV)**

Consider the scripture above and answer the following questions:

In what area of your life is God asking you to look beyond what you currently see and trust Him for something greater?

_____

_____

_____

_____

_____

_____

_____

Have you ever felt God ask you to trust in something that seemed impossible or beyond your capacity? How did you respond, and what did you learn?

_____

_____

_____

_____

_____

_____

_____

Consider Luke 18:27 (NIV): *"What is impossible with man is possible with God."* How does this truth challenge your current perspective on an obstacle you're facing?

_____
_____
_____
_____
_____
_____
_____
_____
_____
_____

Genesis 15:1 (NIV) says, "*After this, the word of the Lord came to Abram in a vision. 'Do not be afraid, Abram, **I am your shield, your very great reward.**'*" Where do you sense God calling you to move—physically, emotionally, or spiritually—that you've been hesitant to follow? What is holding you back?

_____
_____
_____
_____
_____
_____
_____
_____
_____
_____

What could be at stake—not just for you, but for others—if you remain in your comfort zone? How might your obedience unlock blessings for others, just as Abram's obedience brought blessing to many?

_____
_____
_____
_____

_____
_____
_____
_____
_____
_____
_____

Paul instructs us, *"Faith is confidence in what we hope for and assurance about what we do not see"* (Hebrews 11:1, NIV). In what area of your life do you need to act with confidence, even though you cannot yet see the outcome?

_____
_____
_____
_____
_____
_____
_____
_____
_____
_____
_____
_____

CHAPTER 3

UNEXPECTED DREAMS

Dreams without actions can become nightmares.

READING TIME

As you read Chapter 3: "Unexpected Dreams" in *The Fifth Dimension*, reflect on, and respond to the text by answering the following questions.

REFLECT AND TAKE ACTION:

Think of a time when an unexpected situation altered your path. How did you respond, and what did you learn from that experience?

_____
_____
_____
_____
_____
_____
_____
_____
_____

How do you typically respond when life takes an unexpected turn—do you lean into it or resist? What does your response reveal about your trust in God?

_____
_____
_____
_____
_____
_____
_____
_____

> "Remember the instruction you gave your servant Moses, saying, 'If you are unfaithful, I will scatter you among the nations, but if you return to me and obey my commands, then even if your exiled people are at the farthest horizon, I will gather them from there and bring them to the place I have chosen as a dwelling for my Name.'
>
> "They are your servants and your people, whom you redeemed by your great strength and your mighty hand. Lord, let your ear be attentive to the prayer of this your servant and to the prayer of your servants who delight in revering your name. Give your servant success today by granting him favor in the presence of this man."
>
> —Nehemiah 1:8-11 (NIV)

Consider the scripture above and answer the following questions:

Is there a dream in your life that has been delayed or derailed? According to this scripture, what is the contingency for His fulfillment of your God-size dreams?

_____
_____
_____
_____
_____
_____
_____

Where in your life do you need to boldly ask God for His favor, and do you believe you'll receive it?

_____
_____
_____

Reflect on Nehemiah 6:15-16 (NIV): *"So the wall was completed on the twenty-fifth of Elul, in fifty-two days.* **When all our enemies heard about this, all the surrounding nations were afraid** *and lost their self-confidence, because* **they realized that this work had been done with the help of our God**.*"* How would pursuing big dreams with God's guidance and strength set you apart?

James 2:17 (NIV) says, "*In the same way, **faith** by itself, if it is not accompanied by **action**, is dead.*" In your own words, what does this mean, and how does it apply to your God-size dreams?

_____
_____
_____
_____
_____
_____
_____
_____
_____
_____
_____

Have there been moments when you dismissed a dream because it didn't align with your original plans? What would it look like to surrender control and allow God to lead you into something unexpected?

_____
_____
_____
_____
_____
_____

How does the story of Nehemiah encourage you to keep building something meaningful, even when the challenges seem overwhelming?

CHAPTER 4

MISUNDERSTOOD

God-size dreams will always be met with a degree of misunderstanding and jealousy.

READING TIME

As you read Chapter 4: "Misunderstood" in *The Fifth Dimension*, reflect on, and respond to the text by answering the following questions.

REFLECT AND TAKE ACTION:

Have you ever felt rejected or isolated because others misunderstood the significance of your God-size dreams? How did you navigate that experience, and what did you learn from it?

_____
_____
_____
_____
_____
_____
_____
_____
_____

How might others' misunderstanding of your current dreams and visions fit into the larger plan at work in your life?

_____
_____
_____
_____
_____
_____
_____
_____
_____

> "Jabez cried out to the God of Israel, 'Oh, that you would bless me and enlarge my territory! Let your hand be with me, and keep me from harm so that I will be free from pain.' And God granted his request."
>
> **—1 Chronicles 4:10 (NIV)**

Consider the scripture above and answer the following questions:

Jabez asked for an expanded territory despite the challenges it might bring. What "territory" in your life needs to grow, and what challenges are you concerned might surface?

_____
_____
_____
_____
_____
_____
_____
_____

What does this scripture tell us about the size of God's faithfulness measured against the size of our challenges?

_____
_____
_____
_____
_____
_____
_____
_____

When was the last time you shared a dream or vision with someone and felt dismissed? What steps can you take to protect your dreams without becoming discouraged?

_____
_____
_____
_____
_____
_____
_____
_____
_____
_____
_____
_____
_____

Matthew 5:11 (NLT) says, *"God blesses you when people mock you and persecute you and lie about you because you are my followers."* How does this verse encourage you to persevere in the face of opposition?

_____
_____
_____
_____
_____
_____
_____
_____

How do you balance staying true to your dream with staying humble and open to correction from trusted voices?

_____
_____
_____
_____
_____
_____
_____
_____

Consider Psalm 139:1 (ESV): *"O LORD, you have searched me and known me!"* Why is knowing that God fully understands you relevant to your journey through the five dimensions?

_____
_____
_____
_____
_____
_____
_____

Is there a specific misunderstanding or conflict that you need to resolve with someone? How can clarity and open communication help restore that relationship while staying true to your values?

_____
_____
_____
_____
_____
_____
_____

CHAPTER 5

TIME IS YOUR BEST FRIEND

*Obstacles aren't roadblocks;
they're stepping stones.*

READING TIME

As you read Chapter 5: "Time Is Your Best Friend" in *The Fifth Dimension*, reflect on, and respond to the text by answering the following questions.

REFLECT AND TAKE ACTION:

Think of a time when a long waiting period made you question the validity of a God-size dream. How has your perspective of this experience changed over time?

_____
_____
_____
_____
_____
_____
_____
_____

Why is time a necessary part of dream fulfillment? How might waiting serve as protection over the fulfillment of God's vision for your life?

_____
_____
_____
_____
_____
_____
_____
_____
_____

> "But **they who wait for the LORD shall renew their strength**; they shall mount up with wings like eagles; they shall run and **not be weary**; they shall walk and **not faint**."
>
> —Isaiah 40:31 (ESV)

Consider the scripture above and answer the following questions:

How does waiting on the Lord actually renew our strength? What about waiting regenerates our ability to persevere past doubt, discouragement, and hopelessness?

_____
_____
_____
_____
_____
_____
_____
_____

Can you identify a time when the truth of this scripture played out in your life? What do you think God might be doing with that in your journey toward the fifth dimension of dream fulfillment?

_____
_____
_____
_____
_____
_____
_____
_____

How far away does the fulfillment of your God-size dream feel to you? Do you believe there is purpose in what you are waiting for, or does it often feel like wasted time?

_____
_____
_____
_____
_____
_____
_____
_____
_____
_____

Habakkuk 2:3 (ESV) encourages us, *"For still the vision awaits its appointed time; it hastens to the end—**it will not die**. If it seems slow, **wait for it**; it will surely come; **it will not delay**."* Think of a dream or goal that has been slow to develop. What have you learned through the waiting period that you wouldn't have learned otherwise?

_____
_____
_____
_____
_____
_____
_____
_____
_____
_____

Paul charges us in Galatians 6:9 (NIV) to *"not become weary in doing good, for at the proper time **we will reap a harvest** if we **do not give up**."* What "good" things are you doing right now as you wait for the fulfillment of your God-size dreams?

_____
_____
_____
_____

_____
_____
_____
_____
_____
_____
_____

How does the author's story about his encounter with the bully inspire you to push past criticism? What aspects of his approach could you apply to your own situation?

_____
_____
_____
_____
_____
_____
_____
_____
_____
_____
_____

2ND DIMENSION

FAILURE OR BETRAYAL

CHAPTER 6

WHEN FAILURE BECOMES PART OF THE PROCESS

You either pay now and play later, or you play now and pay later, but sooner or later, you have to pay.

READING TIME

As you read Chapter 6: "When Failure Becomes Part of the Process" in *The Fifth Dimension*, reflect on, and respond to the text by answering the following questions.

REFLECT AND TAKE ACTION:

Think of a time when failure unexpectedly shaped your journey. How did it affect your confidence, and did it push you closer to or further from pursuing your dreams?

_____
_____
_____
_____
_____
_____
_____
_____

How have failures in your life revealed hidden lessons or new paths? Looking back, can you see how failure was part of a larger process in your fifth-dimension journey?

_____
_____
_____
_____
_____
_____
_____
_____

> *"If we confess our sins, he is faithful and just to forgive us our sins and to cleanse us from all unrighteousness."*
>
> —1 John 1:9 (ESV)

Consider the scripture above and answer the following questions:

The author highlights how failure is inevitable, but God offers forgiveness and renewal. How does this change your perspective on the weight of your failure or sin as a hindrance to the fulfillment of your God-size dreams?

_____

_____

_____

_____

_____

_____

_____

_____

According to this scripture, God's role is to forgive and clean. What is our role in that process, and how do you see confession fitting into the fifth-dimension process?

_____

_____

_____

_____

_____

_____

_____

_____

When has failure deceived you into believing that you are out of the will of God in pursuit of God-size dreams?

Reflect on Genesis 16:4-5 (NLT): *"So Abram had sexual relations with Hagar, and she became pregnant. But when Hagar knew she was pregnant, she began to treat her mistress, Sarai, with contempt. Then Sarai said to Abram, '**This is all your fault!** I put my servant into your arms, but now that she's pregnant she treats me with contempt. The Lord will show who's wrong—you or me!'"* How does Sarai's attitude misrepresent God's character as it relates to His response to our failures?

_____
_____
_____
_____
_____
_____
_____

To what degree do you tend to wallow or soak in the sorrow of your failures? What should you do instead?

_____
_____
_____
_____
_____
_____
_____

In the book, the author tells a story about a public panel discussion where he felt unqualified but later realized that his greatest fears did not come to fruition. What can you learn from this story and how can you apply that lesson to your own journey?

_____
_____
_____
_____
_____
_____
_____
_____

Proverbs 3:5-6 (ESV) says, *"Trust in the LORD with all your heart, and do not lean on your own understanding. In all your ways acknowledge him, and he will make straight your paths."* In what ways does this scripture provide clarity to how God uses our failures to flourish us?

_____
_____
_____
_____
_____
_____
_____

CHAPTER 7

WHEN BETRAYAL BECOMES PART OF THE PROCESS

*Dreams, often fragile and elusive,
thrive in the fertile soil of adversity.*

READING TIME

As you read Chapter 7: "When Betrayal Becomes Part of the Process" in *The Fifth Dimension*, reflect on, and respond to the text by answering the following questions.

REFLECT AND TAKE ACTION:

Think of a time when someone close to you betrayed your trust. How did that experience stagnate you or cripple you from pursuing your God-size dreams?

_____
_____
_____
_____
_____
_____
_____
_____
_____

How do you typically respond when someone close to you lets you down—do you isolate yourself, retaliate, or seek reconciliation? How might those betrayals reveal the greatness within you?

_____
_____
_____
_____
_____
_____
_____
_____

> *"For it is not an enemy who insults me—I could have handled that—nor is it someone who hates me and who now arises against me—I could have hidden myself from him. But it is you—a man whom I treated as my equal—my personal confidant, my close friend! We had good fellowship together; we even walked together in the house of God!"*
>
> —**Psalm 55:12-14 (NIV)**

Consider the scripture above and answer the following questions:

How has betrayal or broken fellowship with someone affected your relationship with God? What would it look like to trust God again, even when people let you down?

_____
_____
_____
_____
_____
_____
_____

When trust is broken, it can be tempting to isolate yourself. How might you be withdrawing from meaningful relationships because of past wounds?

_____
_____
_____
_____
_____
_____
_____

Is there a betrayal in your life that you've allowed to define your future? How could you take the pain of that betrayal and use it as fuel for something greater than yourself?

_____
_____
_____
_____
_____
_____
_____
_____
_____
_____
_____
_____
_____

Genesis 37:18-19 says, *"But they saw him in the distance, and before he reached them, they plotted to kill him. **'Here comes the dreamer!'** they said to each other."* According to this scripture, it was Joseph's brothers' recognition of Joseph's nature as a dreamer that threatened them. How does this apply to you?

_____
_____
_____
_____
_____
_____
_____
_____

How might the betrayal of others correlate with your God-size dreams?

_____
_____
_____
_____
_____
_____
_____
_____

In Job 19:13-14 (NLT), Job laments, *"My relatives stay far away, and my friends have turned against me. My family is gone, and my close friends have forgotten me."* Read how the account of Job ends. How might your story correlate with Job's?

_____
_____
_____
_____
_____
_____
_____
_____

In Psalm 27:10 (CSB), David says, *"Even if my father and mother abandon me, **the LORD cares for me**."* Where do you see God's care in the midst of betrayal, past or present?

_____
_____
_____
_____
_____
_____
_____
_____

CHAPTER 8

FAILURE IS NOT THE END

Failure provides a crash course on wisdom.

READING TIME

As you read Chapter 8: "Failure Is Not the End" in *The Fifth Dimension*, reflect on, and respond to the text by answering the following questions.

REFLECT AND TAKE ACTION:

Think of a failure that initially felt like the end of the road. How does this chapter challenge that notion? How does it challenge you?

_____
_____
_____
_____
_____
_____
_____
_____

The author described failures that seemed like dead ends but ultimately led to unexpected breakthroughs. Can you recall a personal experience where failure redirected you toward a better path or new opportunity?

_____
_____
_____
_____
_____
_____
_____
_____

> *"For **the righteous** falls seven times and **rises again**, but the wicked stumble in times of calamity."*
>
> **—Proverbs 24:16 (ESV)**

Consider the scripture above and answer the following questions:

What failure in your life do you need to rise from, even if it feels impossible right now? What is one step you can take to get back up?

_____
_____
_____
_____
_____
_____
_____

Pulling from the lessons of this chapter, what are three ways you could adopt the mindset of the righteous—who rise after every fall—to handle setbacks as you make your way toward the fifth dimension?

_____
_____
_____
_____
_____
_____
_____

Psalm 37:23-24 (NLT) tells us, *"The LORD directs the steps of the godly. He delights in every detail of their lives. Though they stumble, they will never fall, for the LORD holds them by the hand."* What do you think the difference is between falling and failing?

_____
_____
_____
_____
_____
_____
_____
_____
_____
_____
_____

In Matthew 6:33 (NIV), Jesus tells us, *"Seek first his kingdom and his righteousness, and all these things will be given to you as well."* Are you pursuing the dream or the Dream-Giver? How do you know?

_____
_____
_____
_____
_____
_____
_____
_____

The author recounts his journey of professional failure, including moments when it felt like quitting was the only option. Have you faced a situation where giving up seemed easier than persevering? What motivated you to keep going (or what would have helped you)?

_____
_____
_____
_____
_____
_____
_____
_____

The book emphasizes that failure is not the opposite of success but part of the process. What are your most recent failures, and how might you frame them as a part of your path toward success?

_____
_____
_____
_____
_____
_____
_____

First Corinthians 15:57 (NIV) says, *"**But thanks be to God!** He gives us victory through our Lord Jesus Christ."* How does knowing that God has the final say assure you that your God-size dreams are still worth pursuing?

_____
_____
_____
_____
_____
_____
_____

CHAPTER 9

WHEN TIME BETRAYS

When time, as a betrayer, interrupts the course of your dreams, don't try to stop the roll.

READING TIME

As you read Chapter 9: "When Time Betrays" in *The Fifth Dimension*, reflect on, and respond to the text by answering the following questions.

REFLECT AND TAKE ACTION:

The author shares the lesson he learned from his motorcycle safety course to not fight the process of delay. What parts of the journey toward your God-size dreams are you fighting? How is it impacting your experience on the way there?

_____
_____
_____
_____
_____
_____
_____

The author discusses the frustration of investing time and energy without seeing immediate results. Are there areas in your life where it feels like your efforts are in vain? What keeps you going during these seasons?

_____
_____
_____
_____
_____
_____
_____

> *"I waited patiently for the LORD to help me, and he turned to me and heard my cry. **He lifted me out of the pit of despair**, out of the mud and the mire. **He set my feet on solid ground** and steadied me as I walked along."*
>
> —**Psalm 40:1-2 (NLT)**

Consider the scripture above and answer the following questions:

What pit are you stuck in right now? How did you get there?

_____
_____
_____
_____
_____
_____
_____

What would it look like for the Lord to steady you right now, even if it meant continuing to endure the discomfort of the process and waiting for the ultimate fulfillment of the dream?

_____
_____
_____
_____
_____
_____
_____

The author shares moments where time felt like an enemy, but those delays ultimately led to growth. Is there a situation in your life where you feel betrayed by time? In what areas do you think God might want you to grow in the waiting period?

_____
_____
_____
_____
_____
_____
_____
_____
_____
_____
_____
_____
_____
_____

Second Kings 8:6 (NLT) describes what happened to a woman whose son had been raised from the dead but had lost her property and was now returning to request it back from the king: *"The king asked the woman, 'Is this true?' . . . And she told him the story. So he directed one of his officials to see that **everything she had lost was restored to her**, including the value of any crops that had been harvested during her absence."* What have you lost that you would like the Lord to restore to you in full?

_____
_____
_____
_____
_____
_____
_____
_____
_____

Reflecting on the author's story, have you ever felt tempted to take shortcuts because you felt that God's promises were taking too long? How did that affect the outcome?

_____
_____
_____

Which dots might God be connecting in your life? What connections do you see thus far, even if you don't yet see the full picture?

CHAPTER 10

LIVING WITH FAILURE AND SUCCESS

Consequences may be your companion, but they will never be your master.

READING TIME

As you read Chapter 10: "Living With Failure and Success" in *The Fifth Dimension*, reflect on, and respond to the text by answering the following questions.

REFLECT AND TAKE ACTION:

Think of a time when you experienced success after a season of failure. How did that success feel different because of the failures that preceded it?

_____
_____
_____
_____
_____
_____
_____
_____
_____

The author describes how success can be just as challenging to navigate as failure. Are there areas in your life where success has created unexpected pressure or challenges? How are you managing them?

_____
_____
_____
_____
_____
_____
_____
_____
_____

> *"So now there is no condemnation for those who belong to Christ Jesus. And because you belong to him, the power of the life-giving Spirit has freed you from the power of sin that leads to death."*
>
> **—Romans 8:1 (ESV)**

Consider the scripture above and answer the following questions:

Are there past failures you are still holding onto, even though God has forgiven you? How can embracing the truth of Romans 8:1 free you to move forward with confidence?

_____
_____
_____
_____
_____
_____
_____

How does knowing that you are not defined by your failures or successes shift the way you approach your dreams and goals?

_____
_____
_____
_____
_____
_____
_____

Read Psalm 103:8-12 (ESV): *"**The Lord is merciful and gracious**, slow to anger and **abounding in steadfast love**. He will not always chide, nor will he keep his anger forever. He does not deal with us according to our sins, nor repay us according to our iniquities. For as high as the heavens are above the earth, so great is his steadfast love toward those who fear him; as far as the east is from the west, so far does he remove our transgressions from us."* As you move through the dimensions toward fulfillment, what is holding you back from fully embracing God's limitless love and mercy?

_____

_____

_____

_____

_____

_____

_____

_____

_____

_____

_____

_____

John 3:17 (ESV) says, *"For God did not send his Son into the world to condemn the world, but in order that the world might be saved through him."* Where in your life are you still living under condemnation, and how would fully accepting Christ's gift of salvation free you to pursue the dreams God has placed within you?

_____
_____
_____
_____
_____
_____
_____
_____
_____
_____

In this chapter, the author shares how even success can lead to complacency if not handled with care. Is there a recent success in your life that may be tempting you to settle or lose focus? What steps can you take to stay aligned with your purpose?

_____
_____
_____
_____

Reflecting on the dimension of failure and betrayal, how have both failure and success shaped your movement through the five dimensions? How can you embrace both as part of God's plan for your life?

3RD DIMENSION

TASTE

CHAPTER 11

IT'S ONLY A TASTE

A taste of what is to come has been given to you as a reminder that the dream is still alive.

READING TIME

As you read Chapter 11: "It's Only a Taste" in *The Fifth Dimension*, reflect on, and respond to the text by answering the following questions.

REFLECT AND TAKE ACTION:

Think of a time when you mistook a "taste" for success. What happened? Did you find yourself underwhelmed by or disappointed in what you believed was the final destination?

_____
_____
_____
_____
_____
_____
_____
_____

How did you respond to the author's assertion that the birth of Isaac was only a taste of the fulfillment promised to Abraham? How does this truth bring clarity to your own situation?

_____
_____
_____
_____
_____
_____
_____

> *"Taste and see that the LORD is good. Oh, the joys of those who take refuge in him!"*
>
> **—Psalm 34:8 (NLT)**

Consider the scripture above and answer the following questions:

Where in your life have you experienced a small "taste" of God's goodness? How has it contributed to the bigger picture of who you know God to be now?

_____
_____
_____
_____
_____
_____
_____

What does this scripture suggest about God's approach to dream fulfillment in our lives? Why does He start with a taste?

_____
_____
_____
_____
_____
_____
_____

The author describes moments when small victories served as encouragement along the way. Are there areas in your life where you've seen these glimpses?

_____
_____
_____
_____
_____
_____
_____
_____
_____
_____
_____
_____
_____
_____

Genesis 15:5 (ESV) says, *"And he brought him outside and said, 'Look toward heaven, and number the stars, if you are able to number them.' Then he said to him, 'So shall your offspring be.'"* Can you identify the "taste" God gave Abraham in this scripture? How do you think Abraham would have fared without it?

_____
_____
_____
_____
_____
_____
_____
_____
_____
_____
_____

How can you accurately assess whether you are experiencing a taste or fulfillment? How should you respond to the taste?

_____
_____
_____
_____
_____

"The Lord was with Joseph, and he became a successful man, and he was in the house of his Egyptian master" (Genesis 39:2, ESV). In what areas of your life are you measuring success by external circumstances? If you were to redefine it, where would you begin?

CHAPTER 12

ON A DIME

To not be fully present is to miss out on the birth of divine dreams.

READING TIME

As you read Chapter 12: "On a Dime" in *The Fifth Dimension*, reflect on, and respond to the text by answering the following questions.

REFLECT AND TAKE ACTION:

The author makes the statement that "to not be fully present is to miss out on the birth of divine dreams." How present are you in the midst of distractions? What might you be missing out on because of lack of presence?

_____
_____
_____
_____
_____
_____
_____
_____

How wide is the gap between the state of your reality and your ambitions? What reminders has God given you that you can hold onto to keep your ambitions alive?

_____
_____
_____
_____
_____
_____
_____
_____

> *"And rising very early in the morning, while it was still dark, he departed and went out to a desolate place, and there he prayed."*
>
> **—Mark 1:35 (ESV)**

Consider the scripture above and answer the following questions:

How does this scripture reveal the power of silence and intimacy with God as a defense against those things that distract you from where God is leading you?

_____

_____

_____

_____

_____

When life feels chaotic or shifts unexpectedly, how intentional are you about seeking God in quiet places? What might God reveal if you made space to pray through the changes you're facing?

_____

_____

_____

_____

_____

_____

Psalm 19:1 (ESV) states, *"The heavens declare the glory of God, and the sky above proclaims his handiwork."* How has God revealed His nature as Creator to you when discouragement was at an all-time high?

_____
_____
_____
_____
_____
_____
_____
_____
_____
_____
_____
_____
_____
_____

Are there areas where you are resisting change because you're afraid of losing control? How might your efforts to stay in control be controlling you?

_____
_____
_____
_____
_____
_____
_____
_____
_____
_____
_____

In Psalm 119:49-50 (ESV), David declares, *"Remember your word to your servant, in which you have made me hope. This is my comfort in my affliction, that **your promise gives me life.**"* What promises has God given you, and how are you allowing the promise to do its life-giving work in and through you?

_____
_____
_____
_____
_____

Reflect on the significance of dimes in the author's life as a steady reminder of God's presence and promises. Have you ever experienced small, seemingly random signs in your life? How might God be using them to guide or encourage you in this season?

CHAPTER 13

CAN YOU BE TRUSTED?

If I did what others did not do, I could potentially get what others did not get.

READING TIME

As you read Chapter 13: "Can You Be Trusted?" in *The Fifth Dimension*, reflect on, and respond to the text by answering the following questions.

REFLECT AND TAKE ACTION:

Think of a situation where you were given a small task that felt insignificant at the time. How did your response to that moment affect the opportunities you were given later?

_____
_____
_____
_____
_____
_____
_____
_____
_____

Have you ever experienced an unexpected promotion? What events led to that, and how might it be traced back to your faithfulness in what God had given you?

_____
_____
_____
_____
_____
_____
_____

> "One who is faithful in a very little is also faithful in much, and one who is dishonest in a very little is also dishonest in much."
>
> —Luke 16:10 (ESV)

Consider the scripture above and answer the following questions:

In what area of your life do you sense God testing your faithfulness with small things? How are you responding?

_____
_____
_____
_____
_____
_____
_____
_____

Describe how the principle of this scripture has manifested in your own life. What specific responsibility or opportunity do you desire God to entrust to you, and what intentional steps can you take to become the kind of person who can steward it well?

_____
_____
_____
_____
_____
_____
_____

What responsibilities have you been avoiding because they feel too small or unimportant? How might God be using those to shape your character for greater things?

_____
_____
_____
_____
_____
_____
_____
_____
_____
_____
_____

"*The warden paid no attention to anything under Joseph's care, because the Lord was with Joseph and gave him **success in whatever he did**"* (Genesis 29:33, NIV). How did Joseph's heart and actions leading up to this point afford him this kind of unmerited favor?

_____
_____
_____
_____
_____
_____
_____
_____
_____

One of Jesus's parables (Matthew 25:21, NIV) ends with, *"His master replied, 'Well done, good and faithful servant!* ***You have been faithful*** *with a few things; I will put you in charge of many things. Come and **share your master's happiness!**'"* If the joy of fulfillment is something you share with God, what gives you the confidence that He will bring it to pass in your life?

_____
_____
_____

Galatians 6:7 (ESV) says, *"Do not be deceived: God is not mocked, for whatever one sows, that will he also reap."* What are you sowing in your life? What are you reaping?

CHAPTER 14

DON'T SETTLE

Settling often occurs when we prioritize immediate comfort over long-term fulfillment.

READING TIME

As you read Chapter 14: "Don't Settle" in *The Fifth Dimension*, reflect on, and respond to the text by answering the following questions.

REFLECT AND TAKE ACTION:

Think of a time when you were faced with two options—one that looked attractive, and one that felt uncertain but required faith. How did you make your decision, and what did you learn from the outcome?

_____
_____
_____
_____
_____
_____
_____

The author emphasizes that not every good opportunity is God's best. Is there an area in your life where you feel tempted to choose what looks easiest or most appealing? How can you discern whether it's truly from God?

_____
_____
_____
_____
_____
_____
_____

> "Brothers, I do not consider that I have made it my own. But one thing I do: **forgetting what lies behind** and straining forward to what lies ahead, **I press on** toward the goal for the prize of the upward call of God in Christ Jesus."
>
> —Philippians 3:13-14 (ESV)

Consider the scripture above and answer the following questions:

How does focusing on the future promises of God help you avoid the temptation to settle for second best? How does this apply to a specific situation in your life right now?

_____
_____
_____
_____
_____
_____
_____
_____

What does "pressing on" look like in your current season? Is there an area where God is calling you to persevere, even though the progress feels slow or unseen?

_____
_____
_____
_____
_____
_____
_____
_____

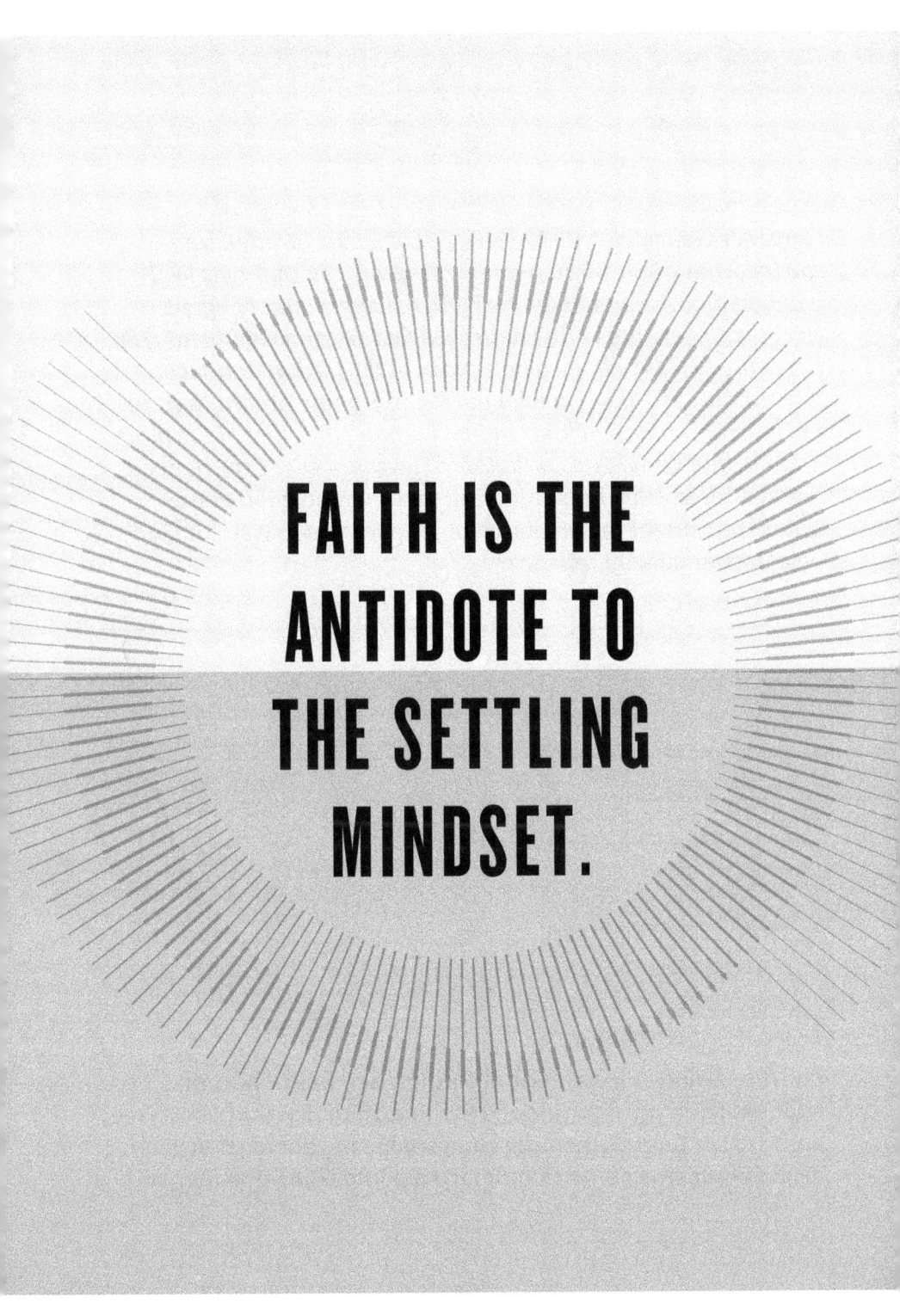

Consider Genesis 13:10-12 (NIV): *"Lot looked around and saw that the whole plain of the Jordan toward Zoar was well watered, like the garden of the LORD, like the land of Egypt. (this was before the LORD destroyed Sodom and Gomorrah.) So Lot chose for himself the whole plain of the Jordan and set out toward the east. The two men parted company: Abram lived in the land of Canaan, while Lot lived among the cities of the plain and pitched his tents near Sodom."* Have you ever experienced regret after settling for something that seemed good at the time? How might that experience prepare you to wait for God's best in your current season?

_____
_____
_____
_____
_____
_____
_____
_____
_____

Ruth's decision to leave behind comfort and follow Naomi required faith, but it positioned her to experience God's best (see Ruth 1-3). Is there something comfortable in your life that you need to walk away from in order to step into God's greater plan?

_____
_____

What practical steps can you take to discern between what is good and what is God's best for your life?

CHAPTER 15

UNCOMFORTABLE PLACES

We can either hoard our resources or allow them to flow through us for greater impact.

READING TIME

As you read Chapter 15: "Uncomfortable Places" in *The Fifth Dimension*, reflect on, and respond to the text by answering the following questions.

REFLECT AND TAKE ACTION:

The author shares personal stories about stepping into uncomfortable situations that stretched his faith and character. Can you recall a time when discomfort led to growth in your life? What did that experience teach you about yourself and God?

_____
_____
_____
_____
_____
_____
_____
_____

Is there a situation in your life right now where you feel God is calling you to embrace discomfort rather than avoid it? What might be waiting on the other side of that challenge?

_____
_____
_____
_____
_____
_____
_____
_____

> "Blessed is the one who perseveres under trial because, having stood the test, that person will receive the crown of life that the Lord has promised to those who love him."
>
> —James 1:12 (NIV)

Consider the scripture above and answer the following questions:

In what area of your life are you facing trials or challenges that feel overwhelming? How can you shift your perspective to see them as opportunities for growth and blessing?

_____
_____
_____
_____
_____
_____
_____
_____

Are you relying more on your own strength than God's to get through a difficult situation? How so, and how is it impacting your ability to persevere?

_____
_____
_____
_____
_____
_____
_____
_____

Reflect on Romans 12:1-2 (ESV): *"I appeal to you therefore, brothers, by the mercies of God, to **present your bodies as a living sacrifice**, holy and acceptable to God, which is your spiritual worship. **Do not be conformed to this world**, but be transformed by the renewal of your mind, that by testing you may discern what is the will of God, what is good and acceptable and perfect."* In your own words, what does it mean to present your body as a living sacrifice as it relates to conformity?

_____
_____
_____
_____
_____
_____
_____
_____
_____
_____
_____
_____

Consider Genesis 22:1-2 (ESV): *"After these things God tested Abraham and said to him, 'Abraham!' And he said, **'Here I am.'** He said, 'Take your son, your only son Isaac, whom you love, and go to the land of Moriah, and offer him there as a burnt offering on one of the mountains of which I shall tell you.'"* What is the significance of Abraham's response to God's calling in the context of seeing your journey through to completion?

_____
_____
_____
_____
_____
_____
_____
_____
_____
_____
_____

Reflect on the five dimensions the author outlines. How has navigating discomfort helped you move through these dimensions toward fulfillment?

_____
_____
_____
_____

Meditate on Luke 9:24 (ESV): *"For whoever would save his life will lose it, but whoever loses his life for my sake will save it."* In what ways are you trying to "save" or control certain areas of your life out of fear of losing them? What consequences have you observed as a result?

4TH DIMENSION

OBEDIENCE

CHAPTER 16

FINISH WHAT YOU'VE STARTED

*Your past mistakes will not
derail your future fulfillment!*

READING TIME

As you read Chapter 16: "Finish What You've Started" in *The Fifth Dimension*, reflect on, and respond to the text by answering the following questions.

REFLECT AND TAKE ACTION:

The author describes the temptation to quit midway through the journey toward dream fulfillment. What are you tempted to quit? Why? What would it take for you to stay the course?

_____
_____
_____
_____
_____
_____

The author references how Abraham prohibited his servants from traveling up the mountain with him and Isaac to prevent them from talking him out of what God asked him to do. Is there someone in your life whose influence or discouragement is tempting you to give up on what God has called you to do? How can you deal with that pressure in a way that is honoring to God and keeps you focused on your God-size dream?

_____
_____
_____
_____
_____
_____
_____

> "And I looked and arose and said to the nobles and to the officials and to the rest of the people, 'Do not be afraid of them. Remember the Lord, who is great and awesome, and fight for your brothers, your sons, your daughters, your wives, and your homes.' When our enemies heard that it was known to us and that God had frustrated their plan, we all returned to the wall, each to his work."
>
> —Nehemiah 4:14-15 (ESV)

Consider the scripture above and answer the following questions:

This scripture describes how Nehemiah and the people of Jerusalem dealt with opposition while rebuilding the city's walls. Can you think of a time when God has frustrated a plan opposing the work He called you to do?

_____
_____
_____
_____
_____
_____

Who or what in your life depends on you finishing the work you've started, and how can that inspire you to press on?

_____
_____
_____
_____
_____
_____
_____

The author describes how resistance often increases as we get closer to breakthrough. Have you experienced this kind of resistance? How did you respond, and what will you do differently next time?

Where might you need to recalibrate your plan or strategy to continue making progress through the five dimensions?

_____
_____
_____
_____
_____
_____
_____
_____
_____
_____

James 1:4 (ESV) says, *"And let steadfastness have its full effect, **that you may be perfect and complete**, lacking in nothing."* What does God's perfecting work look like as you face opposition on your way to fulfillment?

_____
_____
_____
_____

Colossians 3:23-24 (ESV) tells us, *"Whatever you do, **work heartily**, as for the Lord and not for men, knowing that from the Lord **you will receive the inheritance as your reward. You are serving the Lord Christ**."* How aligned is your current level of obedience with the path God has set before you toward fulfillment?

CHAPTER 17

NUMBER TWO PERSON IN A NUMBER ONE WORLD

When circumstances are less than ideal, you still get up, dress up, show up, and refuse to give up.

READING TIME

As you read Chapter 17: "Number Two Person in a Number One World" in *The Fifth Dimension*, reflect on, and respond to the text by answering the following questions.

REFLECT AND TAKE ACTION:

The author shares personal stories about seasons where he served faithfully to champion another's success rather than seeking his own. What emotions or thoughts emerge when you consider serving someone else as their number two person before finding your own place as number one?

_____
_____
_____
_____
_____
_____
_____

Have you ever struggled with finding fulfillment in a supporting role while others were in the spotlight? Why do you think that is?

_____
_____
_____
_____
_____
_____

> "Each of you should *use whatever gifts* you have received *to serve others*, as faithful stewards of God's grace in its various forms. If anyone speaks, they should do so as one who speaks the very words of God. If anyone serves, they should do so with the strength God provides, so that *in all things God may be praised* through Jesus Christ. To him be the glory and the power for ever and ever. Amen."
>
> **—1 Peter 4:10 (NIV)**

Consider the scripture above and answer the following questions:

How are you currently using your gifts to serve others, even if it means playing a behind-the-scenes role? To what extent do you wrestle with stewarding those gifts faithfully without seeking recognition?

_____
_____
_____
_____
_____
_____
_____

Is there a specific way God is calling you to embrace serving others more intentionally, even when the role feels unnoticed or unglamorous?

_____
_____
_____
_____

Acts 20:24 (EV) says, *"But I do not account my life of any value nor as precious to myself, **if only I may finish my course** and the ministry that I received from the Lord Jesus, **to testify to the gospel of the grace of God.**"* How do you reconcile viewing your life as insignificant in light of God's mission, while still embracing the inherent value He places on you and the work He has called you to do?

Have you ever been tempted to push yourself into a leadership position before God's timing? How did that experience impact your journey? What did you learn from it?

_____
_____
_____
_____
_____
_____
_____
_____
_____
_____
_____

The author discusses how supporting roles are often training grounds for future leadership. In what areas of your life do you sense that God is preparing you for greater responsibility through your current role?

_____
_____
_____
_____
_____

Consider Ephesians 6:7-8 (NLT): *"**Work with enthusiasm**, as though you were **working for the Lord** rather than for people. Remember that **the Lord will reward** each one of us for the good we do, whether we are slaves or free."* Are there tasks or responsibilities you tend to dismiss as unimportant or mundane? How can viewing them as service to God reshape your attitude and effort?

CHAPTER 18

SACRIFICE

*What we make happen for others,
God can make happen for us.*

READING TIME

As you read Chapter 18: "Sacrifice" in The Fifth Dimension, reflect on, and respond to the text by answering the following questions.

REFLECT AND TAKE ACTION:

The author shares personal moments of sacrifice when giving up something valuable was necessary for growth. What sacrifices have you had to make in pursuit of your God-size dream? What has it cost you? Is it worth it? Why or why not?

_____
_____
_____
_____
_____
_____
_____

How do you understand the intersection between sacrifice and obedience? Use an example from your own life, and describe how it brought you closer to a goal or fulfillment of a dream.

_____
_____
_____
_____
_____
_____
_____

> "And Abraham picked up the knife to kill his son as a sacrifice. But the angel of the LORD called out to him from heaven, 'Abraham! Abraham!' 'Here I am,' he replied. 'Do not lay a hand on the boy,' he said. 'Do not do anything to him. Now I know that you fear God, because you have not withheld from me your son, your only son.'"
>
> —Genesis 22:10 (NIV)

Consider the scripture above and answer the following questions:

What is God asking you to release that feels as valuable to you as Isaac was to Abraham? To what degree do you trust God with that sacrifice?

___

What does God's response to Abraham's obedience say about His faithfulness to use your sacrifices for your good? What does that look like practically in your own life?

___

We read in Genesis 15:6 (NIV) that *"**Abraham believed** the LORD, and the LORD counted him as righteous because of his faith."* How might your story look differently if Abraham had chosen not to believe the Lord at such a critical moment? What does this say about the far-reaching effects of your belief?

_____
_____
_____
_____
_____
_____
_____
_____
_____
_____
_____
_____
_____

In the book, the author shares that some sacrifices feel like losses but turn into blessings in the long run. Is there a recent loss or change that you now see as a hidden blessing? What shifted in your perspective to help you see it that way?

_____
_____
_____
_____
_____
_____
_____
_____
_____
_____

Isaiah 1:19 (ESV) says, *"If you are **willing and obedient**, you **shall eat the good of the land**; but if you refuse and rebel, you shall be eaten by the sword; for the mouth of the Lord has spoken."* What emotions does this scripture stir within you, and why?

_____
_____
_____
_____
_____

Jesus declares in John 15:14 (ESV), *"You are my friends if you do what I command you."* Are you honoring your friendship with Jesus in the way you navigate the ups and downs of the five dimensions?

CHAPTER 19

THE DARKEST MOMENT

You may not have any control over what someone does. But you have control over how you respond.

READING TIME

As you read Chapter 19: "The Darkest Moment" in *The Fifth Dimension*, reflect on, and respond to the text by answering the following questions.

REFLECT AND TAKE ACTION:

What happens when you allow injustice, pain, and darkness to produce bitterness and anger? How does it impact your path toward fulfillment of your God-size dreams?

_____
_____
_____
_____
_____
_____
_____
_____

Reflect on a time when you addressed bitterness properly and a time when you did not. Compare and contrast the outcomes.

_____
_____
_____
_____
_____
_____
_____
_____

> "Even when I walk through the darkest valley, I will not be afraid, for you are close beside me. Your rod and your staff protect and comfort me."
>
> —Psalm 23:4 (NLT)

Consider the scripture above and answer the following questions:

When have you felt God's presence and seen His faithfulness in your darkest valleys?

_____
_____
_____
_____
_____
_____
_____

In the past, what was waiting for you when you arrived on the other side of a dark valley? How does that apply to your current season?

_____
_____
_____
_____
_____
_____
_____
_____

Are there areas of your life where you've allowed fear to take root because of difficult circumstances? What are you afraid of, and how can you harness that fear to secure your victory?

_____
_____
_____
_____
_____
_____
_____
_____
_____
_____
_____
_____
_____

In Psalm 139:11-12 (ESV), King David declares, *"If I say, 'Surely the darkness shall cover me, and the light about me be night,' even the darkness is not dark to you;* **the night is bright as the day***, for darkness is as light with you."* What is your interpretation of this scripture? How does God's perspective of light and darkness apply to your circumstances?

___

___

___

___

___

___

___

___

___

___

___

In John 14:17 (NLT), Jesus says, *"I am leaving you with a gift—peace of mind and heart. And the peace I give is a gift the world cannot give. So don't be troubled or afraid."* Can you recall a time when you experienced the peace of Christ despite facing opposition or trials? What did that peace mean to you in that moment?

___

___

This chapter highlights that our darkest moments can draw us closer to God. How has this truth manifested in your own life, and why is it necessary in the journey towards fulfillment?

CHAPTER 20

ONE MORE ACT OF OBEDIENCE

The God-size vision is always greater than the level of sacrifice we are prompted to make.

READING TIME

As you read Chapter 20: "One More Act of Obedience" in *The Fifth Dimension*, reflect on, and respond to the text by answering the following questions.

REFLECT AND TAKE ACTION:

What does your fight to the finish line, either past or present, look like when you are on the brink of collapsing? What do you want it to look like and how can you ensure that this time or next time is different?

_____
_____
_____
_____
_____
_____
_____
_____

Who do you have in your corner as you prepare for the "home stretch"? Who in your life might you need to spend less time with, and who should you prioritize spending more time with to align with God's direction for your growth?

_____
_____
_____
_____
_____
_____
_____
_____

> "And without faith it is impossible to please God, because anyone who comes to him must believe that he exists and that he rewards those who earnestly seek him."
>
> —Hebrews 11:6 (NIV)

Consider the scripture above and answer the following questions:

What is your initial reaction to the idea that it's impossible to please God without faith? In what ways does this truth align—or conflict—with your current level of trust in God's plan for your life?

_____
_____
_____
_____
_____
_____

How can you continue to earnestly seek God when you feel exhausted from not seeing the results of your efforts? If you were sitting face-to-face with Jesus right now, what words of encouragement do you imagine He would speak to renew your strength?

_____
_____
_____
_____
_____
_____

The author reflects on the cumulative power of small, faithful acts of obedience. Can you think of a time when one small step of obedience opened the door to greater opportunities or blessings? How did that experience shape your faith?

Has God ever called you to a radical act of obedience? How did you know it was God's voice? How did you respond, and why? What happened as a result of your response?

_____
_____
_____
_____
_____
_____
_____
_____
_____
_____

In Romans 4:3 (NIV), Paul challenges the Jews to reconsider their stance on works-based salvation through the evidence of Abraham. It says, *"What does Scripture say? 'Abraham believed God, and it was credited to him as righteousness.'"* On the basis of this scripture, in what ways do you need to redirect your focus so that God may bless your efforts along the way to fulfillment?

_____
_____
_____
_____
_____

_____
_____
_____
_____
_____
_____

Consider what Elijah said to the widow in 1 Kings 17:13-14 (NIV): ***"Don't be afraid.** Go home and do as you have said. But first make a small loaf of bread for me from what you have and bring it to me, and then make something for yourself and your son. For this is what the LORD, the God of Israel says, 'The jar of flour will not be used up and the jug of oil will not run dry until the day the LORD sends rain on the land.'"* The widow gave from what little she had, and God multiplied it. What do you have that you can offer the Lord right now, whether small or big?

_____
_____
_____
_____
_____
_____
_____
_____
_____
_____

5TH DIMENSION

FULLNESS OR FULFILLMENT

CHAPTER 21

IT WAS WORTH THE PROCESS

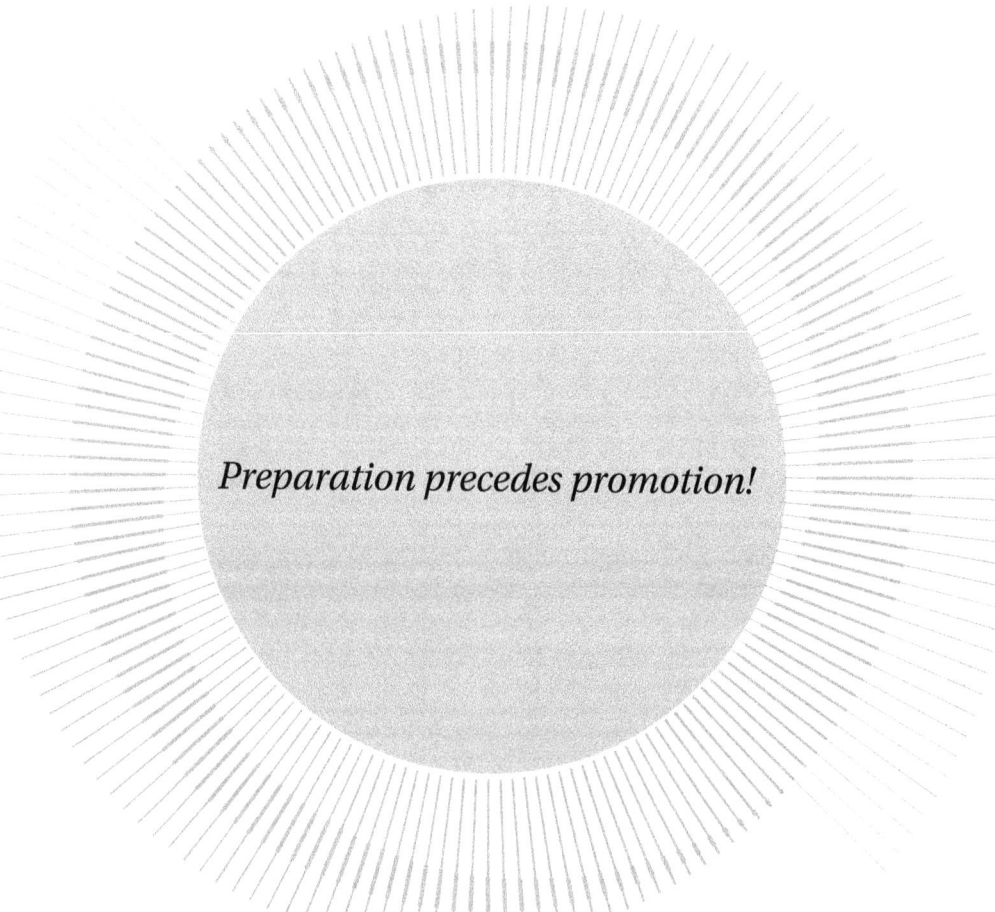

Preparation precedes promotion!

READING TIME

As you read Chapter 21: "It Was Worth the Process" in *The Fifth Dimension*, reflect on, and respond to the text by answering the following questions.

REFLECT AND TAKE ACTION:

The author reflects on how enduring the process often reveals unexpected blessings in hindsight. Can you think of a time when a difficult journey proved to be worth it?

_____
_____
_____
_____
_____
_____
_____
_____

Trace Joseph's journey through the five dimensions and describe why each was necessary before God could fulfill the dream He had given him long ago. What might have happened if Joseph had skipped one or several dimensions?

_____
_____
_____
_____
_____
_____
_____
_____

> *"Let us not become weary in doing good, for at the proper time we will reap a harvest if we do not give up."*
>
> **—Galatians 6:9 (NIV)**

Consider the scripture above and answer the following questions:

What good work in your life has left you feeling weary or discouraged? How can you renew your strength to remain focused and stay faithful to the task at hand?

_____
_____
_____
_____
_____
_____
_____

Can you think of a time when you gave up prematurely? What were the consequences?

_____
_____
_____
_____
_____
_____
_____
_____

Reflect on Genesis 41:41-46 (NIV): *"So Pharaoh said to Joseph, 'I hereby put you in charge of the whole land of Egypt.' Then Pharaoh took his signet ring from his finger and put it on Joseph's finger. He dressed him in robes of fine linen and put a gold chain around his neck. He had him ride in a chariot as his second-in-command, and people shouted before him, 'Make way!' Thus he put him in charge of the whole land of Egypt."* What aspects of Joseph's journey prepared him specifically for this moment of fulfillment? How were his earlier experiences tailor-made for his future assignment, and what does this say about how intentional God is in His work?

_____
_____
_____
_____
_____
_____
_____
_____
_____
_____

What goal or dream do you sense is on the horizon? Why is it worth waiting for?

_____
_____
_____
_____
_____
_____
_____
_____
_____
_____

Consider Job 42:10-12 (NIV): *"After Job had prayed for his friends,* **the LORD restored his fortune and gave him twice as much as he had before.** *All his brothers and sisters and everyone who had known him before came and ate with him in his house. They comforted and consoled him over all the trouble the LORD had brought on him, and each one gave him a piece of silver and a gold ring.* **The LORD blessed the latter part of Job's life more than the former part.***"* How does knowing that the Lord intends to exceed the best you've ever had—provided your persistence through the dimensions—compel you to drive forward?

_____
_____
_____

After reviewing the five principles essential to achieving fulfillment (adaptability, faithfulness, stewardship, connectivity, preparation), which one resonates with you the most? Where do your strengths align, and which present the greatest challenge for you?

CHAPTER 22

GREATER THAN *YOUR* DREAM

When you get out of your way to make other people's dreams come true, God will put people in your path to make your dreams a reality.

READING TIME

As you read Chapter 22: "Greater Than Your Dream" in *The Fifth Dimension*, reflect on, and respond to the text by answering the following questions.

REFLECT AND TAKE ACTION:

The author reflects on how God's plans are often greater than anything we can envision. Have you ever experienced a moment when God's outcome surpassed your original dream?

_____
_____
_____
_____
_____
_____
_____
_____

Are there areas in your life where you've been holding tightly to your own dream? How willing are you to surrender that dream and trust God for something even greater?

_____
_____
_____
_____
_____
_____
_____
_____

> "Now to **him who is able** to do far more abundantly than all that we ask or think, **according to the power at work within us**, to him be glory in the church and in Christ Jesus throughout all generations, forever and ever. Amen."
>
> —Ephesians 3:20 (ESV)

Consider the scripture above and answer the following questions:

What dream or goal in your life feels too big or impossible to achieve? How does this scripture challenge you to believe that God's power working within you can accomplish even more than you imagine?

_____
_____
_____
_____
_____
_____
_____

What are you expecting from God now? Is the expectation too small? Why or why not?

_____
_____
_____
_____
_____
_____
_____
_____

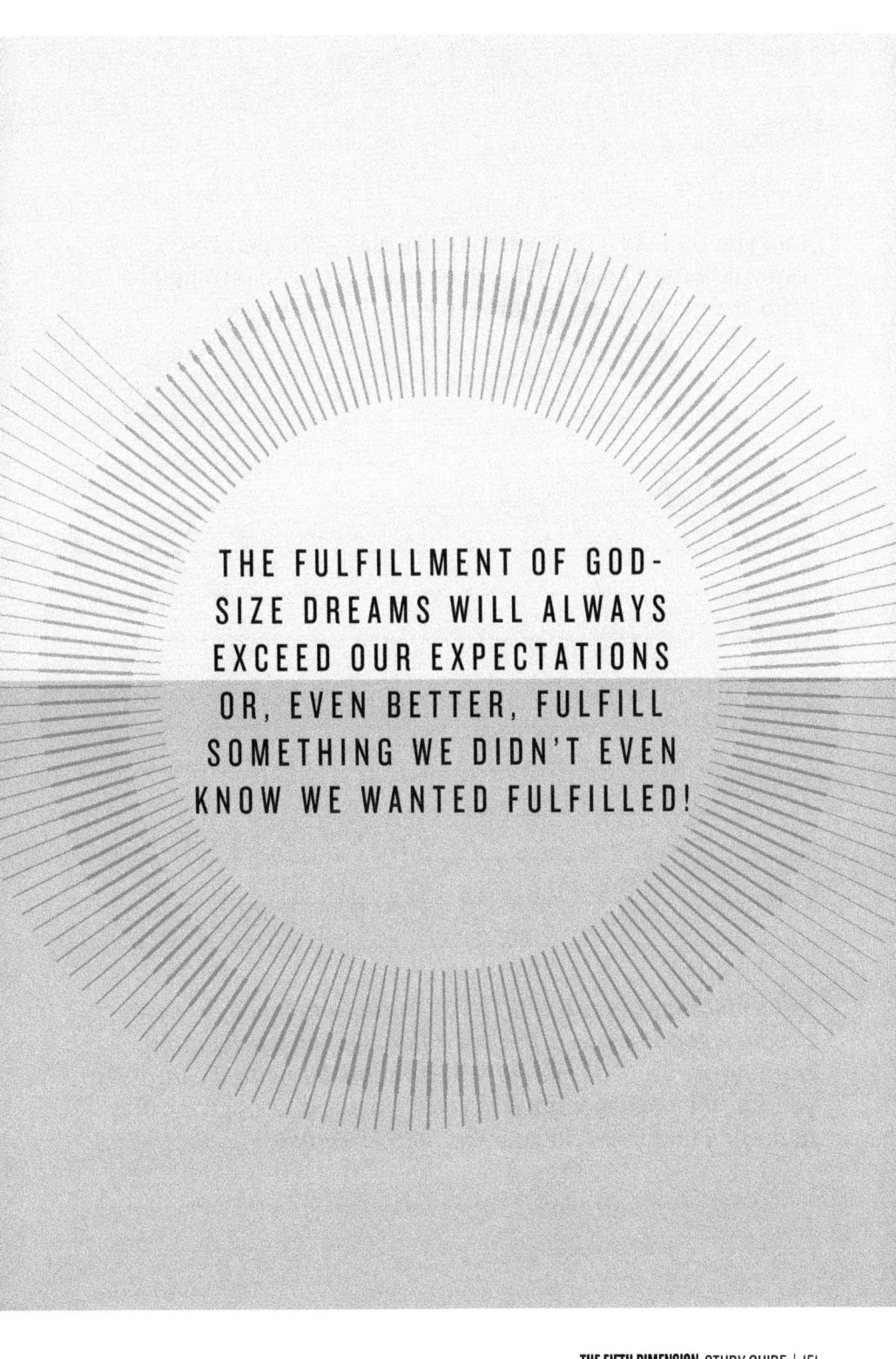

Can you think of a time when God's plan exceeded your expectations? Explain. How does that experience strengthen your trust in what He is doing in your life right now?

_____
_____
_____
_____
_____
_____
_____
_____
_____
_____
_____
_____

Jesus instructs in Luke 6:38 (NIV), *"**Give**, and it will be given to you. A good measure, pressed down, shaken together and running over, will be poured into your lap. For with the measure you use, it will be measured to you."* What role does giving play in finding fulfillment in your God-size dreams?

_____
_____
_____

Why do you think God is so intent on exceeding our limited expectations? How does this aspect of His character paint a bigger picture of who God is and shape us into who we need to be for what's ahead?

CHAPTER 23

WHOSE DREAM IS IT ANYWAY?

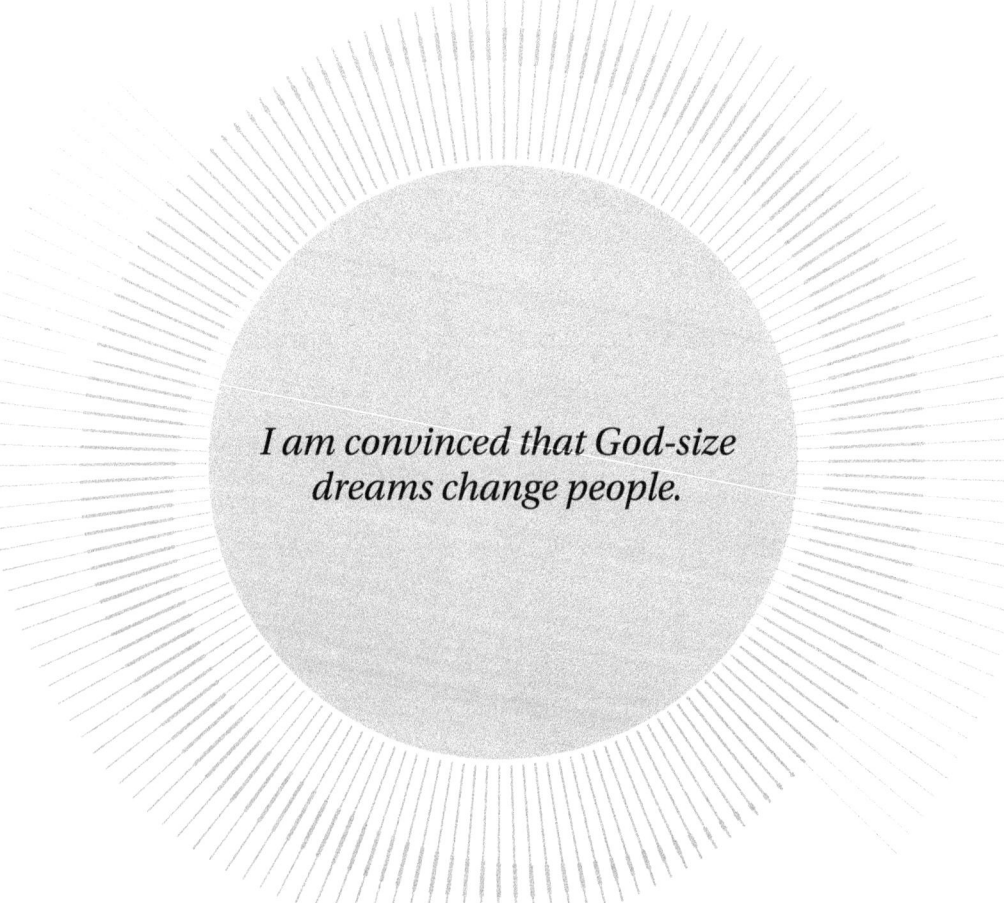

I am convinced that God-size dreams change people.

READING TIME

As you read Chapter 23: "Whose Dream Is It Anyway?" in *The Fifth Dimension*, reflect on, and respond to the text by answering the following questions.

REFLECT AND TAKE ACTION:

In what ways do you look, talk, and walk differently now than you did before, and what did God use in your life to accomplish that?

_____
_____
_____
_____
_____
_____
_____
_____

How has God used others to accomplish a purpose in your life far beyond your own ambitions and desires, similar to how He used the chief butler to promote Joseph? Whom is He using in your life right now?

_____
_____
_____
_____
_____
_____
_____
_____

> "Then Joseph said to his brothers, 'Please come near me.' And they did so. 'I am Joseph, your brother,' he said, 'the one you sold into Egypt! And now, **do not be distressed or angry** with yourselves that you sold me into this place, **because it was to save lives that God sent me** before you. For the famine has covered the land these two years, and there will be five more years without plowing or harvesting.
>
> 'God sent me before you to preserve you as a remnant on the earth and to save your lives by a great deliverance. Therefore it was not you who sent me here, but God, who has made me a father to Pharaoh—lord of all his household and ruler over all the land of Egypt.'"
>
> **—Genesis 45:4-8 (NIV)**

Consider the scripture above and answer the following questions:

What warnings can you heed from this scripture regarding blame, unforgiveness, and resentment as you endure the opposition that comes with moving along the dimensions?

_____
_____
_____
_____
_____
_____
_____

What challenges or hardships from your journey through the five dimensions can you now recognize as blessings from God, and how can shifting your perspective from blame to gratitude transform your outlook?

_____
_____

The author emphasizes that God's dreams are always tied to a larger purpose beyond ourselves. What relationships or communities would your dream impact if you followed it with God's purpose in mind?

Where have you witnessed God's divine wisdom guiding your journey in ways that you know could not have come from your own understanding?

_____
_____
_____
_____
_____
_____
_____
_____
_____
_____

In Acts 17:28 (NIV), Luke writes, *"'For in him we live and move and have our being.' As some of your own poets have said, 'We are his offspring.'"* What about living, moving, and having our being in God relates to His character as the Dream Giver?

_____
_____
_____
_____

What are you waiting to figure out before continuing your journey toward fulfillment? How might taking the next step of faith unlock the fulfillment of your God-sized dream?

CHAPTER 24

FORGETTING THE PAIN

You can't fix your past, but you can set new standards for the future!

READING TIME

As you read Chapter 24: "Forgetting the Pain" in *The Fifth Dimension*, reflect on, and respond to the text by answering the following questions.

REFLECT AND TAKE ACTION:

What memories from your past are you holding onto that are paralyzing you from moving forward? Craft a personalized prayer asking God to heal those areas to free you to receive greater things.

_____
_____
_____
_____
_____
_____
_____
_____
_____

What painful memories of the past have you buried that need addressing?

_____
_____
_____
_____
_____
_____
_____
_____
_____

> *"And after you have suffered a little while, the God of all grace, who has called you to his eternal glory in Christ, will himself restore, confirm, strengthen, and establish you."*
>
> **—1 Peter 5:10 (ESV)**

Consider the scripture above and answer the following questions:

In what ways has your suffering through the five dimensions afforded you greater strength?

_____
_____
_____
_____
_____
_____
_____
_____

How can you speak to the temporal nature of your suffering, given the promise outlined in this scripture?

_____
_____
_____
_____
_____
_____
_____
_____

Reflecting on the five dimensions, how has each step of the process prepared you for this final stage? What specific lessons will you carry forward as you move into this new season?

Genesis 41:51-52 (ESV) says, *"Joseph called the name of the firstborn Manasseh. 'For,' he said, '**God has made me forget all my hardship** and all my father's house.' The name of the second he called Ephraim, '**For God has made me fruitful** in the land of my affliction.'"* Describe how healing from a specific hardship yielded great fruit in your life and lay out your vision for what that would look like now.

_____
_____
_____
_____
_____
_____
_____
_____
_____
_____
_____

Psalm 34:17 (ESV) declares, *"When the righteous cry for help, **the Lord hears and delivers them** out of all their troubles. The Lord is near to the brokenhearted and saves the crushed in spirit. Many are the afflictions of the righteous, but the Lord delivers him out of them all!"* What is crushing your spirit, and what needs to happen to overcome that oppressive hurdle?

_____
_____

What in your past would you like to leave behind, and what new standards would you like to set for the future?

CHAPTER 25

READY FOR ANOTHER CYCLE?

You do not go back to the beginning. Instead, you grow from the beginning.

READING TIME

As you read Chapter 25: "Ready for Another Cycle?" in *The Fifth Dimension*, reflect on, and respond to the text by answering the following questions.

REFLECT AND TAKE ACTION:

In your own words, describe the five-dimension process and detail how it works. Why is it not linear but rather cyclical? What evidence from your life do you have of the cyclical nature of the dimensions?

_____
_____
_____
_____
_____
_____
_____
_____

If you have come to your fulfillment, what is next for you? If not, what do you sense God is preparing you for after the fulfillment of your dream?

_____
_____
_____
_____
_____
_____
_____
_____

> "So on that day Moses swore to me, 'The land on which your feet have walked **will be your inheritance** and that of your children forever, because you have followed the LORD my God wholeheartedly.'
>
> "Now then, just as the Lord promised, he has kept me alive for forty-five years since the time he said to this Moses, while Israel moved about in the wilderness. So here I am today, eighty-five years old! *I am still as strong today* as the day Moses sent me out; I'm just as vigorous to go out to battle now as I was then. **Now give me this hill country that the LORD promised me** that day. You yourself heard then that the Anakites were there and their cities were large and fortified, but, the LORD helping me, I will drive them out just as he said."
>
> —Joshua 14:9-14 (NIV)

Consider the scripture above and answer the following questions:

Based on your current state of mind, how willing are you to keep following the Lord, even when faced with challenges and hardships?

_____

_____

_____

_____

_____

What can you learn from Caleb's confidence in his faithfulness to the Lord and his standing as a rightful recipient of God's promise? Of what has God deemed you a rightful recipient, and what will you do to align your reality with that promise?

_____

_____

Meditate on 2 Corinthians 3:18 (ESV): *"And we all, with unveiled face, beholding the glory of the Lord, are being **transformed** into the same image **from one degree of glory to another**. For this comes from the Lord who is the Spirit."* What does it mean to you personally to be transformed from one degree of glory to another?

Numbers 23:19 (ESV) says, *"God is not man, that he should lie, or a son of man, that he should change his mind. Has he said, and will he not do it? Or has he spoken, and will he not fulfill it?"* How does this scripture challenge the doubts you hold against God today?

_____
_____
_____
_____
_____
_____
_____
_____
_____
_____

Now that you are familiar with the nuances and features of the five dimensions, in which dimension do you find yourself now, and what actions do you need to take to keep moving forward?

_____
_____
_____
_____
_____

What are three action steps you can begin to take today to support your advancement toward the fulfillment of your dream in accordance with your present position along the fifth-dimension process?

CALL TO SALVATION

The Bible tells us in Romans 10:9 (NIV), *"If you declare with your mouth, 'Jesus is Lord,' and believe in your heart that God raised him from the dead, you will be saved."*

God's love for you is unconditional, and His desire is for you to experience eternal life through a personal relationship with Jesus Christ. No matter where you've been or what you've done, His arms are open, ready to receive you. Today, you can step into the life God has for you—one filled with forgiveness, purpose, and hope. All it takes is faith and a willingness to receive His gift of salvation.

If you feel a stirring in your heart to surrender your life to Christ, you can respond right now through this simple prayer of faith:

Heavenly Father,

I come before You today with an open heart, ready to receive Your love and forgiveness. I confess with my mouth that Jesus is Lord, and I believe in my heart that You raised Him from the dead. I surrender my life to You, trusting that You have a plan for me that is good.

Forgive me for my sins and make me new. Fill me with Your Holy Spirit so that I can walk in the fullness of life You have promised. Help me to trust You every step of the way and to follow Jesus all the days of my life.

Thank You for Your grace, Your mercy, and the gift of salvation. I declare that I am now a child of God, saved by Your love. In Jesus's name, I pray. Amen.

If you prayed this prayer sincerely, the Bible assures you that you are saved. Welcome to the family of God! We encourage you to connect with a local Christ-centered, Bible-based, Spirit filled church or faith community to grow in your new relationship with Christ.

Blessings today and always!

Printed in the USA
CPSIA information can be obtained
at www.ICGtesting.com
CBHW070701081224
18564CB00007B/23